TORN
FROM THE
SUN

TORN FROM THE SUN

GREGORY DONOVAN, *1950 –*

 RED HEN PRESS | *Pasadena, CA*

Book design and layout by Nicholas Smith and Michelle Olaya-Marquez

Library of Congress Cataloging-in-Publication Data

Donovan, Gregory, 1950–

 [Poems. Selections]

 Torn from the sun / Gregory Donovan.—First edition.

   pages cm

  ISBN 978-1-59709-326-2 (softcover : acid-free paper)

 I. Title.

 PS3554.O548A6 2015

 811'.54—dc23

                              2014037133

The Los Angeles County Arts Commission, the National Endowment for the Arts, the Pasadena Arts & Culture Commission and the City of Pasadena Cultural Affairs Division, the Dwight Stuart Youth Fund, the Los Angeles Department of Cultural Affairs, Sony Pictures Entertainment, and Ahmanson Foundation partially support Red Hen Press.

First Edition

Published by Red Hen Press

www.redhen.org

ACKNOWLEDGMENTS

Grateful acknowledgment is given to the publications—and to their editors—that afforded initial publication to the following poems, sometimes in alternate versions:

32 Poems, "Erasures"; *42opus*, "Ravens at Tamalpais," "Sleepwalker in the Medicine Wheel," "Sputnik as Holy Ghost," "Triumph of the Will as Underwater Ballet"; *64 Magazine*, "Belle Isle"; *Alaska Quarterly Review*, "Strange Child," "Winter Solstice Oregon Hill"; *Chautauqua Literary Journal*, "Quipu of the Scorched Lord"; *Connotation Press / Congeries*, "The Great Fire of Smyrna," "Standing before Shiva as Lord of the Dance," "The Visit: Clouds in Trousers"; *Copper Nickel*, "After the Fire and the Big Bang and All That," "Night Hours in the Office of the Dead"; *Crazyhorse*, "Besides," "The blue breath in the red branch"; *diode*, "Angel of the Waters," "Milagros," "Portrait of the Artist with Columbus in Chains"; *Fives: Fifty Poems by Serbian and American Poets, A Bilingual Anthology*, "Aliens Are Calling Us Away"; *GSU Review*, "Breathing in the Cool"; *Gulf Coast*, "Portbou: Walter Benjamin at the Border of Dream," "Taste"; *Hayden's Ferry Review*, "Another Offensive Discourse on Love and Marriage, with Fireworks," "Cattle Kate"; *MiPOesias*, "Oracle on 42nd Street"; *storySouth*, "Is There a Dead Mule in It"; and *Triquarterly*, "Instructions for the Labyrinth" and "Night Train for the Bardo of Auvers."

"Is There a Dead Mule in It" is for David Raffeld.
"South African Woman of 1986" is in memory of Nelson Mandela, 1918–2013.
"Sleepwalker in the Medicine Wheel" is for Dennis Kevin Donovan, 1955–2004.
"A Thanksgiving in Mountains with Kensei and Wind Chaser" is for Keith Alan Donovan, 1963–2014.

The author owes a debt of gratitude to the College of Humanities & Sciences of Virginia Commonwealth University for a leave in which to complete a final draft, and to Max & Mary Ann Cisne for their continuing support. For inspiration, encouragement, and advice my endless thanks go to Norman Dubie, David St. John, David Wojahn, T. R. Hummer, Beckian Fritz Goldberg, Anna Journey, Peggy Shumaker, and in all ways to Michele Poulos. Many ongoing thanks to Kate Gale, Mark E. Cull, and all at Red Hen Press for giving this manuscript its chance at life.

FOR MICHELE,
WHO OFFERED THE THREAD

CONTENTS

[ONE]

[T W O]

[T H R E E]

ONE

Did he have the labyrinth in his head?

—TOMAS TRANSTRÖMER

AFTER THE FIRE AND THE
BIG BANG AND ALL THAT

things changed. Photos curled up and lost face, metals shifted
color, trophies melted, glass crackled, wood whistled and sang.

All along, that roar. Fingerprints on my right hand disappeared
onto an unsuspected knob, the other side of the door nothing

but tongues of fire. I stood with a garden hose playing
water without hope against the kitchen ceiling. It was bleeding

tiny flames. Something crawled by. Human. Two of the kittens
died despite heroic efforts. Sirens. Uniforms. They fooled me

into the ambulance. They laughed and said *did you fight
the fire*. Man. My head up there in the surging pull of black

again. I had to *lay down* they said *you'll be all right if you don't
cough up black*. Laughing without smiling, wrapping my hand

in gauze. To get away I held back until they let me go. On the way
out, blinking into the restroom's fiercely mirrored white, I coughed up

black. So what do we have here. You lit a candle for me to clear
the air as I worked. Then out for a brisk walk into Easter Sunday.

What's that sound we said. *Why are those people
running*. It all went down slow motion. What couldn't be saved

went up in seconds. The universe is constantly expanding,
dark energy pushing us apart at ever-increasing speeds.

They say the echo travels out with us and never goes away.
Dante's skull has undergone facial reconstruction, and he looks

better than expected. The latest theory holds that we are one
universe among many. Nietzsche thought it might all go on again,

and forever. After all, given the infinity of the past, if the universe were
finite, it would already have ended. Many unhappy returns for every

one that's good. I was a victim of smoke. After the fire
we fade to black in roaring winds. You are forgiven. No one could

get back the boy who burned, get back home on wings turned to ash.

❧

RAVENS AT TAMALPAIS

Bald white trunk & dead black bark, *toc-toc*. Small shrugs
in long black coats, their stripped pine whipping at the skyline . . .

swiftly unveiled in twos and threes, ravens and the ideas
of ravens slip out onto air, black silk scarves

pulling each other through the silk blue sleeves
in wintry sky & out into the mind's eye to stall and dip,

nip at tail feathers, roll and dive, flip, spin, fold up
and fall, one thing after another in that sleight of hand

to alight again, pinned to their pine towering above the bay,
the smashed hat of Alcatraz floating. *Turn my cold face to your sun.*

Alarm calls, chase calls, flight calls, wing whistles,
bill snaps—and among their clacking & clicks

comes a ceaseless mimicry of our human speech, *talk talk*
they have captured on the wind, on the wing,

and as the far white city sinks back into its fog
they speak for us in lost languages, confused tongues.

The 'alalā of Hawaii, extinct in the wild, live only
in cages now, the Pied Ravens of the Faroe Islands

parade as museum stiffs, yet here, these ancients blown down
& off course & away from ancestors in ice age Asia

swirling in a blizzard rage two million years gone, these strong
settled Tamalpais long before the word arrived.

In Sweden they were glass-bottomed boats, airy ghosts
of the newly murdered dead, while in Denmark they fed

on the hearts of kings and still could read thoughts of men
before men themselves could think them.

Within the eye of slaughter, the raven's eloquence.
And who will love me when I'm gone?

Ravens will call coyotes and wolves to the work,
to tear open the carcass for shaggy birds to feed upon.

A raven forgets nothing and is a most skillful thief
who brings away the shining and the bright,

black-eyed poets stealing each other's buried cache and
flying farther and faster to hide what was stolen.

A raven showed Adam how to scrape the dirt for Abel,
and yet *I have slept* as ravens slid down steep banks of snow

to take off again into the dizzying loops of their delight.
I have slept as the sacred spies of Odin, his eyes and ears, his ill

memory and blunt mind, flitted down to swallow anything at all.
Bird of Prophecy, Bringer of Fire, Protector of the Tower,

Groom of the Daughter of the Fog whose soft touch
on ocean's hair will lure salmon to leap into the boat:

your mother swallowed the white stone, smooth as an egg.
Toc-toc. Your cry is the knock at my coffin door.

If I step up now to that highest trail's edge and slip
off and flap my puny nightmare wings and cry out

in the long fall, *then you will hold me* in the last dark
of your glance, fly to me, cure me, take out my eyes. *Toc-toc.*

TASTE

When she put her finger inside
his mouth, there was Hispania
and the dusty roads pocked
with droplets of rain before
the wooden wheels came grinding,
the impassable suck of black mud.
When she put her finger inside
herself again, he was there, too,
taking the famous Spanish steps
into the foothills among the azaleas,
they were building the sunlit villa
to which they would always return.
When she put her finger inside
his mouth, there was the temple
and the hands clapping sharply
against the steep stair, bringing back
the call of the quetzal, the star
shining in her dark eye,
the blood running down the stone.
When she put her finger inside
herself again, he was almost
there, but she did not come
that night, nor the next,
and another rung on the ladder
that led to—where?—had broken
as the stars faded, the bright birds
disappeared, the walls fell in,

and she never came to him that way again.
When she put her finger inside
his wounds, he knew them all
once more—she said she found it
hard to believe all they had told her—yet
he knew if she would believe, in that moment
he would be healed for as long as the mockingbird
sang, as long as the taste nailed him down
or gently wrapped him up and took him away
to a story that wouldn't die in a world without end.

NIGHT TRAIN FOR THE
BARDO OF AUVERS

Drawbridges over the Seine   steam up and down

levitating   over long fly boats that ply the flashing

waters   which all day transport oil slicks of guilt

and all night   spin black whirlpools of doubt.

The approach in a glass-ceilinged boat is   looking up

toward yellow frames   of passing window lights

and then I am   there, aboard the rail coach, looking out.

The milky whorl of night   folds its arm

over its face   in the heart of the sky, its hurt

palm curled in, crucified   with the hard sharp spike

of a single white church spire.   Boiling clouds

mass   along the horizon, climbing its stair

of blue mountain.   A bottle-green cypress twists

in its struggle against the pull   of burning stars

that wheel not   far above in the cloudy sky. Breathing

smoke   and black as coal, the heavy locomotive

has broken from the dark   to drag its cars

along   through roiling mists so thick and quick

the train appears   to rush backwards

and I am given to know   my suitcase has been

left on the platform   back at the sad eternal station

and though I am now   amazingly returned

for one like me   who has tried to slice off his own

head   I have been electrified with color

and among so many   rows upon rows of drab lifeless bags

I can no longer say   which one is my own.

BREATHING IN THE COOL

John Coltrane, there on the edge
    of a red morning, leans on the sill
of an open window, breathing in the cool
    wind that pours over his shoulders—

the air mixed with some rare,
    complex smoke, a taste of plum
and pepper, as the song makes itself
    ready in him. He fingers the instrument
sleeping in his hands, the pads pop,
    the keys clack, until the song grows taut
and restless, until it has to be let go.

He will follow it on. The song turns
    down an alley, slips downstairs, lies
on its back in the dark and will not move.
    But it crawls out, gets back on its feet
in the middle of the street. When it goes
    strutting downtown, looking for trouble,
it is going wherever the hell
    it has to go, and it rolls on
in the might and rumble of thunder.
                 Deep
    into it, in the heart of its fog,
there
    where nothing can be held down

or numbered or stolen, where nothing
can be salvaged or hauled back, there,
    at that depth where you can tap
                    the perfected
emptiness at the center of its making,
    he finds its spirit breath hovering
right there beside him in the room.

It is a lemon-colored light,
    and now it begins to dance and slowly
to blossom.
              It is heavy water,
    the clear flower splashing back into itself
after the stone.

It is a tree feeling out to find
    its every possible root and limb.

It is death—someone else's death—
    at the moment you hear of it and know
that same death will be your own.

It is the mother of all knowing—
    everything you have known and forgotten
until the song plays it out again.

It lives at the edge of invention
    and it means to go on and on.
He believes it would like to kill him.
    And what in the world does it want?

It wants *elegance*.

That is all, and it is all
    that can save him, it is all
that can take him up.

As the song finishes, the light
    gathers itself. It flies into the bell
of the horn and vanishes
    into the mouth and throat
of John Coltrane where it will live on,
    making it back through song after song,
coming back to kill him one more time.

ANGEL OF THE WATERS

Stone-cold sober when the silver angel appears
    On Bourbon, you fall in. *Religion is for boneheads*
Who won't take a drink
    Unless someone leads them to water

Your demented friend once said laughing and even Rilke
    Whispered *every angel is terrifying.* But you fall in.
You give yourself that shadow-shuffle along Decatur,
    That see-through ramble past the Old Absinthe Bar.

The she-males at the Black Cat Club won't arch
    A penciled brow—she strolls a soft shoe over
Mardi Gras gumbo paving the cobbles, chipped
    Pedestal slung under her arm, wings trembling.

The angel won't hurry or pause . . . her half-smile stops
    Tourists passing by and *they* stumble, she seems
So lost. We're drawn into the wake of her dream:
    The *Vieux Carré*, a storm blown from Paradise.

Verily this day will be nothing like the movies. She doesn't zoom
    To a library, place her light hand on a shoulder, tap
Into the steam. She hangs listless on no trapeze.
    No armor and no bell, she stands there, waiting to become

Stone, skipped into the lake of the mind's eye and you, blue ghost,
    Leave her to the murmur of the crowd gathering

In the square to watch and wait, each one looking
        For the smallest tic or wink to betray

What she could be under that silvery alien skin.
        Hour upon hour she brings down the strong
Spring sun, almost smiling. Bets are taken.
        Small offerings are tossed in the overturned hat.

Los Perdidos—worshipped in Mexico, the newspaper says, survivors
        On rainwater from the bilge, who gnawed seagulls & sea turtles.
289 days with Chava's Bible & mad Lucio on air guitar.
        They saw the angel twice, toxic as seawater, walk the open waters.

Milagro. You've come back to see. She's moved into the shadows
        Of Pirate's Alley and its magnolia park where duels whirl on
In the dust, where drunks have labored and screwed themselves
        Up in garrets, writing the way out of desire. You fall in.

She steps down from her rickety stand and you
        Follow, second-lining down the way of sorrows, and while
You stumble and you burn, she won't look back,
        Not until you have passed beyond

The edge of the Quarter, where the angel stops.
        You stand beside her to look into that face.
When the illusion shatters, its stone and steel release
        Someone with tattooed shoulders and a nose ring,

A pierced nipple and a past. Once she was an actress,
    A little dancer, once she was somebody's daughter
Running down the moonstruck hall of a house silent as
    All of bloody Kansas now. *That girl*, she tells you, *is dead.*

You discover your body in this cloudy noon, the dead girl gone
    Into the angel again, stranding you flayed with hunger,
Flaked with thirst, with scattered stone and shattered steel,
    The temple veils torn, the curtains flying, that thunder rolling in.

PORTBOU: WALTER BENJAMIN AT THE BORDER OF DREAM

False Morpheus, god of the bruised testicle, god of the ivory gate
and the blackened eye, he lives on in nothing more than this
dust pressed on the tip of a finger, taste bitter and strong
as all that's gone wrong. It may still blow away in one puff
of breath, in the consonant beginning of the last word of his last
Project. The arcades empty out, objects fall asleep, they begin again
to vanish, the mirrors multiply each other's empty faces
as the customers and idlers there slowly erase.

He turns from his preparations for the voyage
to the black briefcase beside him and this final book
he'll carry to the top of a sinking mast, more dear
than his own life. Once again the guards at the border
have not let him pass, there is clearly no way out,
the Nazis have his number, they are working on his face.
His bags are packed and lost forever, and now within the sun's
low slant, it does not seem so much this thing he has done.

Quick, he opens an evaporating briefcase in the imagined arcade.
He sees them again, in the blotters of his exercise books:
the puzzled labyrinths a boy has drawn there. *Not to find
one's way in a city is of little interest, but to lose
one's way, as one loses one's way in a forest,
requires practice.* He has learned his last art too late
in this walk of life. The mountain passes of the Pyrenees
are filling up with snow, filling up with chalk and bees.

Far to the south, a man is drawing mountains of morphine
onto a piece of rough, white handmade paper—
a pensive man, for whom these Alps are the portals of birth—
the man must be Borges, sketching the twists of a thick
black line crossing itself again and again, a lifetime of footsteps
traced into a tangled nest, but now it's late, the project has gone
wrong, his pain has eased, so he crumples himself into a small,
cruel ball, flicks his wrist once, and lets go of it all.

CATTLE KATE

"... big cattlemen took the law into their own hands [and on]
July 20, 1889 a group of them lynched James Averell and
Ella Watson near Independence Rock."

—T.A. Larson, *History of Wyoming*

Four crows, all at once. Three magpies,
                    one at a time. Every living thing
          a body might see through the gap
taken up and held in the eye,
                    like God keeping count of all
          the damned little sparrows. And now these
seven jaybirds dark as winter morning shadow,
                    they're up to something, they don't squawk.

          One of them would be that cowboy
last spring. I let him watch me
                    from behind as I cooked so he could
          do what he needed right there
but it was pie on the table, not me,
                    the bawl of the steer he paid with
          getting mixed up with the little whine
he gave finishing up. That maverick outside
                    the window sniffed and nibbled
          at the leaves of the crabapple
until I shouted. Maybe it doesn't matter
                    now but you know I gave them all
          the same deal: immediate payment—
cold cash or livestock—and wearing
                    no man's brand, like me. That cowboy
          was hungry, like the rest, & quick.
I felt sorry for them all.
                    I didn't think of him again

until just this minute. Slipping
that marked card into the deck.

When I look over at Averell,
                his face isn't right. It's hard
            to remember him as the only man
who ever took his time with me.
                    We sat under cottonwoods and yellow
            leaves poured down in the wind
like October would never end.
                    Now they've got that sack
                over his head, too. He doesn't look
like anyone I've ever known.

I sniff at the chaff and sneeze.
                    One of them says, "Hey there Missy, allergic
            to rope?" and slips it rough and thick
over me. Is this worse than the worst thing
                    you could imagine? *Damned old
            cattle-thieving whore.* They've got to
call you that if they want to kill you.

Old Bothwell, he sits off there, watching.

Here it is July and I'm shivering.
                    It's like the wind that blew three days
                that November, like someone talking

and talking and you can't believe
                 they won't shut up. Then it snowed.
         James Averell showed up the third night,
nearly frozen. We kept each other warm
                 all that night, saved our lives.
         We never rustled any cattle.
Applied for our own brand five times,
                 they turned us down, the big boys
         closing us out. Then that damned steer.

They're going to string us up right
                 close so we can dig and kick
         at one another until the show is done.
Bothwell's promised he'll have everything
                 we ever owned. I know he'll burn
         my house. My scrawny tree that counts
the birds on its fingers.
                 That crabapple has the prettiest
         white blossoms in spring.

TRIUMPH OF THE WILL AS UNDERWATER BALLET

Rites for an American November

The shaman finds a mirror carefully slipped
beneath the water of a running stream
will open a window in the land of the dead.

Here, the yellow and umber leaves, doom boats
strapping the current, slip quickly over the dappled
bottom where rusted wheels and bent scaffolds backdrop
The Triumph of the Will as it simmers there, bubbling,
awaiting the buoys of resurrection.

Here and there the camera winks its dark eye.
It cannot forget anything it has seen fit
to take into the black box of its mind.

So the film spools out and smooth-cheeked
Nazi faces yearn up and up like limbs tendered
outstretched against the sky, sky branches filled
with bread and circuses hovering over
the purling curl and useless talk of the river,
whisper-road for shipping slaves home
to the backbone of stone broken off just there
from the mother continent and drifted
through all the ages it took to become just this
breakdown of falls at Richmond, now, here.

Riefenstahl, young or old, might have known
what to make of it, how to see things right.

The German Cleopatra is *the Queen of Denial*?
Ninety and frail, she does not flinch
when the shark darts in to bump
its nose against her own in its rubber mask.
Another triumph, lifting the heavy
camera in the water's dark. Her bright
smile engages no arrogant evasions.

And there I am, too, looking back up
from the bridge shivering under the river, not waving
a flag or pulling a gun but making myself
take a hike here in the mind-sweeping cold
alone. Here I am again leaning on the rail
where I focused my dead brother's field glasses on
the pointed yellow-grey beak, the fierce gold-red eye
of the great blue heron, who glanced upstream
fitfully, then turned back once to look at me.

The heron sees whatever is there and saw
something that took something black and no bigger
than a book from the pack on its back
and held it a while. Then threw the tape in.

The river rising today wants to say it this time—
push it names itself and what it wants
push and holds to it, hesitates only
a moment before the dip and pour

over and down like polished dark glass
into the white splash and froth which
uttered in twisted tongues of current
returns eternal to the same stretch of rock.

Courage may be to see whatever is there.
The river speaks faster now here and there
where stone gathers and hunches, *push*
against the geese who have come again
to swim against the current in pairs *push*
and shake their tail feathers into the air to duck
down for the choice morsel, to reach
down for whatever is there.

Riefenstahl would know, she always responded
to the magic opera of the fairytale spell,
the marching throngs, the sweet muscle
and magnetics of its surging pull, the unstoppable
vine crawling, the drama of evil, its hydraulics
precise, the attractions she would never deny.

So they all go down in the water, flipping
once and twice, flashing, spinning, and soon
the smiling Nazi formations are in the swim
of their underwater Berlin, artfully turning
with synchronized grace. It must be hard holding
their breaths and smiling always smiling and pretending

to sing from the bottom of their hearts
from the bottom of that sea and *selling it*,
their magnificent ballet, until it all settles
in the silt, bottoming out here and there,
those bubbling songs still hanging on their lips
as they go down and away, the plazas dim, the ritual
dies down and is emptied and is done,
a chorus of lies answered with lies,
the mirror cracks, the window slams shut.

In Egypt once we thought the sin-drenched sack of the heart
could be balanced against the feather of truth,
and those heaviest hearts would be chewed to bits
as the lighthearted stepped onto eternity's deck.
We wrapped ourselves up and we waited.

Now the river rushes by, faster now, pushed on
by heavy rain on the far mountain we can't see,
saying what it's said for so long we can no longer hear:

shh—one long lazy hush, its wobbly bubble
rising to break—*shh*—opening to a release without end—
never the same river, never the same never
and never again—*hush now, shh.*

THE GREAT FIRE OF SMYRNA

The city is burning again. The page lies open,
      smoke rises, boiling up, screams held within.
O sudden ones, phantasms, denizens of the air.

The city burns. Turkish soldiers throw oil into the houses.
      Thousands mass on the waterfront. Stampeded, beaten,
robbed and raped. Many leap into the sea.
      We struggle to hear them at this distance.
O daimons, slippery ones, tritons and gorgons.

The bazaars burn, smoke unfurls at the horizon's lip,
      the page turns. Bodies float on the waves
so thick you could walk over the water.
      If a swimmer reaches for the neutral ships,
sailors are ordered to chop free the hand.
      Ikons in the churches sweat their tears of lead.
O roaming ones, apparitions, visions that pass by.

And what will we do when the weariness steals
      over us like fog rolling into this harbor?
O false ones, banished ones, devils and satyrs.

Ashes smolder in bulged heaps, the bodies are stacked.
      The photographs will not cease their staring.
All our gods are hidden, drifting off in smoke.

MILAGROS

Chula Vista, California, 1991

into the night air sweet and cool
pouring out mums and roses
red silk ribbons Lourdes water
a child's pretty toys the saints
fire in their eyes painted on tall
veladoras people kneel to light
bread broken onto small white plates
that knock at the door she answered

when the big shots take away
the lights we put them back
even if we have to steal them
from the Marlboro Man when dark
comes now she appears
many people have been healed
thousands by the wall of prickly pear
fat paws to slap yourself awake
they stand there watching crazy
goddamned Mexicans the anglos say
they think it is all in our minds yes
it is in all our minds nothing
nothing but night in their caved-in
skulls when the helicopter beats down
its white eye beating down over
the gathering people like Hollywood
cops moving in hard damn your eyes
nothing matters now but when

the shadows on the empty billboard
begin to swirl like gathering dust
up there in the *barrio* sky she has a way
of coming back to us
to warn us *ask for something*
say her name
Laura Arroyo murdered nine-year-old
translated into heaven bearing my name
we are to look for who
stole her the children are still
in danger who is this people
ask phone calls from the dead
I will comb her black hair straight
se cuenta el milagro pero no el santo
yet the killer's name will be told

she will not eat dirt like me
the billboard blacked out three nights
the other world is rising again
when I bring my mother's comb
bone for the bone world I bear
it I am a big woman yes I will bear
up under his cross he has slipped
off down the Boulevard of Hell
carrying that pickaxe on his shoulder
but I am standing here and I see

PORTRAIT OF THE ARTIST WITH
COLUMBUS IN CHAINS

Born 1451, of disputed origin. Sent home in chains, 1498.

Cabrón, we were born to travel cuffed to the numbers, the not-yet
     forgotten years of the rotten centuries in whose middle we were conceived.
Prisoners of our names & days, we might never slip the bone ache, waking
     hard in the stiff ligaments of every unbelieving morning,
the slow cold drizzle, the smell of wet iron,

except those few moments we might look straight in the eye
     of some foreign face, handsomely formed, smooth-browed,
and what do we see gathering there, cloudy with hope?
     They have their gods, and they are not among us. We are lonely
and abandoned again. What face for an incensed god hiding in smoke?

Death there makes his little clink and clank turning over
     to remind us. We wait for the sun to come again
and loosen every joint. Remember the tall Asian-eyed woman,
     her thick black hair, her voice a spiced balm so smooth
it raised every stubborn scar? She sang us to sleep, it changed nothing.

We fight on, slap our swords onto the waves, but sailors
     steer badly and time is wasted, asses bray and we are sentenced
to listen. *Milk and honey.* What do they know of finding such
     gold? May hurricanoes sink them heavy with treasure.
Admiral of the Ocean Sea, you and I have come to discover

the great water is no pale nimbus, no blank sheet to etch
     with a name, not a bucket to piss in, and all maps lie. What good
were our puny green flags and those charters written

in tears and blood? We brought them death, they gave it back.
Our errors have made us. We might end up buried anywhere.

Carve what you wish into the tombstone, it's lies upon lies.
    Let us not be confused forever, anointed one, in the texts of dirt & rock.
The sea's the place to be. We'll taste the water, test its salt
    to see how far we are from land.

STANDING BEFORE SHIVA AS
LORD OF THE DANCE

St. Mungo's, Glasgow

The wheel of flame keeps spinning and so it must
have been my turn for the demon of ignorance
to slip up behind me on a buckled city sidewalk
in the blackwater ebb of night, lost in those depths
of my wandering away from home, away
from the woman I had left so beautifully
angry and alone, adrift on our bed's floe.

He asked directions to a mumbled crossroads
that did not exist, and so I did not just then
recognize him as the churlish Apasmara
even when he showed me the length
of pipe which would bust my skull,
he thickly explained, if he didn't use
the gun he had tucked under his sweatshirt.

I made him follow me out into the lava
of leaf shadow shivering down the middle
of the street so that if I was clubbed or shot
at least I would be found before morning.
He took my wallet, money, and ID, and left me
hopping one foot to the other, waiting
to run as he shouted over his shoulder,

Don't you move. Then, *I know where you live.*

Too late, here in another country, another tick
of the wheel, caught flat-footed before this lithe cast
of gunmetal tall as me, I see now what I could have done:

               I could have danced,
keeping my head erect, rolling my eyes,
holding the hourglass drum in one hand, the fire
in another, making my four hands into the sign
of the bone house, the sign of life-from-death,
making the sign *do not fear*, making the sign
there is a way out. I could have lifted

my left foot with the poise of the elephant breaking
a path through the jungle, breaking through the encircling
flames, and whirling fast as Shiva under the half-moon
streetlamp, could have spun on the demon's back, smashed
the god particle, shattered the mojo, escaped the illusion,
a snake uncoiling from my right arm,
my desires in ashes, rivers of stars in my hair.

TWO

I am not a man, I am dynamite.

—FRIEDRICH NIETZSCHE

INSTRUCTIONS FOR
THE LABYRINTH

Abandoned in that maze, raised by those walls.

Quarry must be, from the start, to hunt
the raw block you seek, the translucent
skin, the span without fault, the clear
milk-white eye of myth. Stone that will hold
and keep. Trace the fissure and pound it
with iron wedges jammed between iron splints
hammered with iron-headed mallets. Follow
the spreading fissure as if you tracked
the story of your birth. Open it
for the levers and with so many hands
as can be found, push. You will not
want the story, you will want sleep.
Split it from the parent rock. Finally
the deep-throated crack, the massive release.

Cut away the excess and flip it
for leveling. A river rises now
in the mountains of your birthplace
from a dark cavern in a vast chain
of underground streams and caves.
You have been told. Save the polishing
for later; there may be damage
along the route. Ropes, pulleys, winches.
Levers, beams, and rollers. Muscle it.
It must be raised from the hole.

The uncle who tried to strangle you
to silence was no uncle at all,
not even *friend*, but stranger.
Even now you talk too much,
using words to grease the skids.

Maneuver it from the sledge
onto the heavy wagon with the tall
wheels. Hitch up the mules.

Again you travel to the reputed house
of your birth. The rooms unfold
into other rooms. No one knows you there.

Hoist the load up the incline,
sending down the mules yoked
to the empty wagon as the other wagon
rises. Set the chocks. Again.

You were sent away at birth
to be raised by strangers.
Mother and *father*, in the spill of time.
That procession of hidden stars.

Cast sand over the marble face and rub
down with the smoothing plate.

Grind for days. It will take two of you,
more if they can be found.

And when you find your way back again
your birth mother at last will deny you.

The assembly must be seamless
and follow the plan of the double
axe, the seed pattern refined.
Set your mystery in its navel.

Then will come the sacrifices,
the bull leaping, the bull fights.
The dancing. The woven mosaics underfoot.
The wine. The king on his throne.
The quake and flood. The erosion.
The mirrors and confusions of blank
moonlight, the statues that walk.
The genius free or merely lost in the tumble,
black water flowing out over the land.
The broken gate swinging wide
onto the sizzle of emptiness, where there is
center everywhere, no circumference at all.
The scream of its hinge to ride in your eye
torn from the stone, torn from the sun.

SPUTNIK AS HOLY GHOST

Born under the sign of Stromboli, wrinkled
As the face of the two-thousand-year-old man,
Skin cap tied with braided thong beneath his
Little chin, pulled from the bog with forceps, Ingrid
My mother, my father a guy who lived in the sky.

Slipped naked and barefoot out of The Iron Age
Into the 1950s cold and war to be shipped
Upriver, Moses in reverse, to be raised
By a Booneville schoolgirl and the military police.
A garage apartment with dirt floor and rats
Watching me in the cage of my crib watching them
Being shot from its bars by my good mother and her rifle
With the bone sight, a deadeye leaving that indelible
Mark on the soul of the small soldier of Christ, a baptism
In blood. The Stone of Scone disappeared
Into Scotland. Rockets launched. Seven years on,
More sacrament lasered down from the glittering bird
In outer space. I arrived at the speed of fantasy and despair
At inner space and the age of reason under the sky-spark

Of Sputnik's cycling eye. I was asked to pledge
My life to the preservation of capitalism and
The Catholic Church. I had already swallowed Jesus.
O the Sputnik, oowah, it sang my name, it sang
My papery-whispery name: Baby Bleep. Baby Bleep Bleep Bleep.

MILE HIGH CLUB

Air pressure

       blood pressure

              Pressure of moods

A feeling

       of falling

              after

Waiting for the path

       to clear

              watching

Avoiding

       the eye

              Anything to keep from

The oiled palace of onyx

       dreamed up

              shining cold

Wheeled in

       to keep anything to keep

              from spilling

The long

       path twisting up

              the mountain

Don't misstep

      don't slip

            down

The door from

      outside buckling

            ready to enter

The feel of it smooth

      flying

            bump

Bumping into

      unexpected

            sensations

Kept from you kept

      from you all this

            blasted time

Wings inside

      wings outside lift

            and dissolve

Smoothed

      above the clouds

            to keep from

If this was about sex
              it's all eaten up
                        with ambition & desire

Beautiful foolish arms
              enwrapping
                        unwrapping

Reversals of altitude
              letting it happen
                        blacking out

Into a pleasure and fear
              of falling
                        of being done

CITY OF CROCODILES

She laughed and in that whisper so like the swift soft beat
of a crow's wing
                            she captured her friend Marguerite
where she sauntered among the boulevard's monkey shadows,
saying her husband was gone to his boys and his dogs
therefore they would be adventuring together that night
and now here was that indispensable remedy in top hat, M. Black
the hysterically named undertaker who was always turning
up in that silk chapeau simmering with ghastly ghostly faces
to provide her with the yellow powder she sprinkled
into her cigarette and, disappointing him again, she spun
into her friend's arms to pinch her nipple and say
I have heard of a place in the country,
                                    a farmhouse
of ill repute where anyone may find anything
so desired and we shall see what may be on offer
for us there, and raising her finger she waved as if
flicking a wand and the hansom cab stopped and they were
off.
        They arrived in moonless dark and considerable
confusion—Marguerite had disappeared and she found herself
in the quiet hallucination of the barn where an octagon of rough-hewn
boards encircled a raised bed of fresh straw and as she shed
her outer garments by the amber light of a single lantern to lie down
and sleep a dark-haired young man, distracted yet well-dressed,
appeared.

His hand entered hers and he entered her
and they commenced for hours tenderly and without a word
to ring the changes.
            In the end she felt a wet warmth against her neck—
his tears or tongue—and he was gone.
                        She rose to dress, dimly
recollecting—the wink of a gold band on his finger?
                        And there it lay
on the planks of the crude bedside table, nestled within the ball
of crumpled banknotes he'd left. She angrily ripped and tossed them
into the troughs of dark in the orchard rows lining the road for home, cursing
brothers dead in their muddy wars and husbands drifting like those drowned
trees turning over in the river,
                        as if an exhausted swimmer flailed out
with a crooked arm, wooden and damp yet soft as ashes when touched by the dawn
she witnessed as she stepped down from the farmer's cart onto the white
bridge over the Seine. Yet instead of dropping the thing into the amber water's
chop, she slipped its gold onto her thumb and wore it to the grave.

ANOTHER OFFENSIVE DISCOURSE ON LOVE
AND MARRIAGE, WITH FIREWORKS

Let's say right off we may have invented this point of view purely
so that no one could be found talking here at all. Fields
of tall grass could turn red with cold, or burn, murders
of crows row south, snow drift over the mountain, & it wouldn't be anything

personal. Let's say we even drag in some tattered watermark of an *I*
to tell an antique tale of romance: *The long-nosed gods of December shook*
the bamboo in their icy hands. Supple stems dipped and swayed through the chill
black depths of winter sky, confusing the stars, and I took you for my own.

It couldn't hurt. Depending on the season and your dose of weariness or vanity,
the X or K you've swallowed in your education, force-fed—you might choose
sarcasm for one, identify with the other. Choose a vowel. That little old *I*
could be laughing or weeping and it would have nothing to do with little old *U*.

We slept in the glassed-in solarium, above us white jointed culms
pitching and tossing, strange to each other under the clack of icy branches
that first holiday in your ancestral home. All of us lying still
and awake in the cold. Quiet, slow, the two of us made ourselves one.

But we know there was no *we* and they made nothing. Nothing now
that couldn't erase itself inside the sad jingles and plastic Santas riding
the air like bad bubbles, along with the nothings huddled in the snowy pine,
two house sparrows perched on a branch nearby, shivering as we passed.

Nothing that summer couldn't make tinseled and absurd.
Let's say you climbed to the roof to read and lie in the angry sun
alone. Let's say I crawled into the dark under the house
and wouldn't come out even when you called. Let's say it all.

Or we could pinch this sick rhetoric and slowly bend it around, bring
down the branch to wire it, and if it snaps, the birds will merely flit away
with one last *cheep* and swiftly enter the silence of paper sky
and be gone. So we can erase and safely forget. All the *you's* and *I's*.

What's a pronoun but a noun less famous?
And what's a marriage but sulfur & charcoal rolled into saltpeter
and packed tight into a tube of paper to be set on fire. Oohs and ahs.
The *Time Rain*, the *Glitter Palm*, the *Diadem*, the *Cake* and *Ring*.

Now the damned author has disappeared into smoke. He walks a beach in Mexico
in a white suit, stares beyond the frozen waves like a penitent barefoot in snow.
He is painting himself into an impossible scene, perhaps. But can we tell
anymore if he's the one thinking: *what is pain or pleasure, but a single vowel?*

NIGHT HOURS IN THE
OFFICE OF THE DEAD

Slow current meandering the dark before dawn. A glimmering
water-self called up *from the depths*
                           into the dreaming rush
tumbling along downspout to gutter, to enter now as the simple
rain. He ascends like a lost balloon to drift through the thick
fabrics of his dark, reaching out a hand, testing
with his toes for territory that's shifted, the seven mysteries
that surface in a moment's flood . . .
                         He hath delivered
my soul from death . . . my feet from sliding
                           He stands weak
in the canticle of icebox light to take his medicine,
bitterness most bitter
                 which eats hollows through his
feeling sorry for himself without the headlamp of shame.
Vespers, compline, matins, lauds. The hours go by
like boxcars, preoccupied. A last wisp of wet smoke
snakes past when the white door snaps shut holding its one
snapshot, a boy's uncertain grin above the orange
breast of wet lifejacket, itself the resisted sign of joy
rising in the motorboat's rising bow, the churn of lost
time frothing the wake trailing behind them, his face
thrust forward into all the wet wind and water
of the silvered river to come.

Thou shewest thy might, and persecutest dry stubble

The cicada still sings in its tree. *Mercy,*
he hears, *mercy me.*

                 He lives in the space between,

naked in his blue skin gone gold, tattooed
with leaf-shadow and bars of the blind
now crossing this page toward you as the rain begins
to stop. The wind stirs, the trees sigh, droplets
trouble the street's black-banded pools. Like us,
they wish to speak with him now, too late.

And let perpetual light shine upon them

He charms the traffic away awhile longer;
the empty scene is his to mind. Engines hum
near and far—but not here, not yet. He trusts his face
to his hands, closes his eyes, and dreams a rooster
crows. But a pair of headlights cuts through his fingers,
then another. He loses his hold on the morning, accepts
he cannot wait on the wrath of day with that soprano
singing deep in his ear where the fever throbs.

Suffer me therefore, that I may a little
lament my sorrow, before I go, and return not
unto the dark land

The stoplight shuffles through
its three colors, a light grows in the east
under a bird's cry.
      My soul doth magnify

the wind. The violin comes again into his hands
but he cannot reach the music that's needed. He turns
from the window to the empty bed *replenished*
with miseries.
      The bird song has ceased. The last clear note
evading him through all his scorched hours, the single
falling drop releasing many voices—plink—*from the morning*
watch even until night
              a clarity awaited   an echo   a blink

only now will it stop playing

hard to get.

IS THERE A DEAD MULE IN IT

. . . there is indeed a single, simple, litmus-like
test for the quality of Southerness in literature.

What say we throw off the narrative
imperative this once and let the damned mule
live—and why not—let him live on with the spirit of Fidel
in his sensitive hairy lip and his long white tooth,
the power of Ali in every hoof,
the sting of a hornet in his rump?

Let's take this chance to drive it deep
into the Carolina piney woods, into that light
flashing its potential for migraine and epileptic
fit as black trees fly by, where we're supposed to pull
a paint job for the wilted Southern branch
of the family Rockefeller, & we'll find him
there, that inescapable crazed gallop
barreling at us, that excitable suicidal reincarnation
of Che kicking up the gravel road, and so
the resisted and shattered story may begin again,
& in it I, in dubious first person,
will barely get the fishtailing
truck stopped in time
to avoid killing him
outright, to say nothing
of the farmer running right
behind him, though I had to
swerve broadside & the mule jumped
up into the back of the pickup,
wreaking havoc with the paint,

splattering his long dark legs
Dead Canary Yellow
and the back window cracked, not
from the mule but the hammer
the farmer had whipped
from its holster in his bibs
and fired at the mule's head
to get him to *by God dammit now
stop*, but you know he wouldn't?

(Thus the story, now in color, may carry on in glory.)

Place my partner there riding shotgun,
a Jew from Chicago, wandering grandson
of rabbis of Poland and Russia, and he will
sit there stunned as any Yankee at Bull Run,
but the loping farmer, he has put me in mind
of my own grandfather so I will slip out
& in a smooth flanking action, quietly
enter the past tense and wave
my arms once & the giddy
mule who was mighty limber for one so old
will have bolted gamely for home and farted twice
in time-honored traditional revolutionary salute
by the time the farmer swings the moaning gate shut.

Some things never change, I said.
The farmer didn't say a thing,
but looked as pleased
as a farmer can look
who has on his hands
among other tribulations a *wild mule*
as the man's own story will soon have it
*what leaps over fences
and jumps into trucks.*

The farmer pulled out his wrinkled
wallet but I refused, it was just the one
crack, the International Harvester
pickup was old, and the Rockefellers, they
could afford one more gallon
of that damned yellow paint. Besides,
I told him, we would all get something
out of this. A story. We would call it
The Battle of First Mule Run.

*Well he's a yellow-bellied
sapsucker now for sure.*
The man said this without a grin.
He was no Rockefeller on your TV.

And we could end it all here,
a postmodern polyvocal fragment but

this bunch of Rockefellers
for whom we were going to work still
owns even now several solid square miles
back there, a little kingdom of pain
with its own post office, though
once they owned even more,
including all the red clay and pines
to make your Fort Bragg.

Some things never change.

The job was to paint up a special
heated indoor pool, a giant Dead Sea
thrashing bath of surging alchemical waters
and steam that up close roared as if
God was in there bubbling somewhere
but it was only Mrs. Rockefeller
who had the arthritis in her
special aquatic room that had been lined
with exotic soundproofing tiles—
the third set, actually, replacements
imported from Italy—so that
when you dropped a hammer right
there beside the pool, it could not
be heard on the other side.

My mother is there on the other side,
she told us once, *she rode a white horse in gloves.*

Into the clean Danish dressing rooms
with a sprig of mint from the garden,
seventy years the family retainer,
and all his people slaves before that,
a tall man in bow tie and white monkey jacket
carried us iced tea in the hot afternoons.
We got him to bring himself a glass,
sit down for it, and when he was told
my partner was a Jew from the North,
he refused to believe again. *Naw*, he said,
waving his long thin hand, *all y'all are kin.*

By this time the Rockefellers
had sold all their mules.

I can picture the old lady there still
floating deep in the heart of whispering
waters. I imagine her God is in there, too,
waiting for her in the steam. He has taken
the form of an angry mule.

My painting partner has gone back
to Yankeeland, back to rooting
for the curséd Sox and being

devout, an officer in his synagogue,
fatback gravy and biscuits for him no more.

And whatever the *I* represents or obstructs
in self-delusion or narrative transparency,
I am still sweating it out in the South,
and yet here I have managed to tell
you this story, like a miracle,
with only one lie.
              Because as you well know
some things never change, and although
they may live in their impotence
forty years in some cases or longer,
all stories, even broken ones, come to *la fin*,
& given his talents and bold predilections,
his taste for rebellion and soured corn,
it must be that by now in cold & hard truth,
bless his heart, that poor mule
named Robespierre is surely dead.

ERASURES

With the fog snaking in and pocked
With strangers adrift, with my feet dissolving,
Then my knees, and the wading through waylaid ghosts,
Burked cadavers for the anatomy classes of Dr. Knox,
With the acidic rain in my eyes beading my lashes,
With the prickly wind and low evening sun,
With the portrait of Stevenson still an agony,
Bronzed consumptive hung on the cathedral wall

Sitting up in bed with that smoking pen in hand forever
On the Royal Mile, yet coughing out his time in Samoa
With its five rivers and its mountaintop under a *flying cloud*
And his yearning all his murdered life to get back
Home to slip again into his shadow pacing Edinburgh's fog
Swirling there yet in its bad damp, waiting to rub him out.

Tusitala, storyteller. With the mockery of his gravestone
Copied on his plaque—*Home is the sailor, home from the sea*
And with the toes of my boots soaked black
And my collar wet and cold on my neck,
Considering his American bride, Fanny,
Whose wit followed and nursed him over the seas,

I kept on walking away from the inn with its *tweedle-de-dum*,
And yet I swore to pack all of it back home with me
Along with the chilled pain in my feet and the ache
In my legs, the wildlife I never saw, the little I did,

And so I stood there in the footpath, looking
Hard. Yet when it cleared, it was the view

Of the river that hurt most. It was a Bonnard
View, cypresses on the far bank brooding
Over the shadowy water as it surrendered
Its light, the long grasses gone blonde, the small
Gargling stream wandering across there and down
Through the choking reeds and glittering brush,
The decision out of nowhere
To add the woman in a yellow bonnet,

Almost not a woman at all, just a bit
Of color, walking away up the hill into the dark.

RED SKIRTS

The uncle and the brother scratch
                              at themselves and pull
          on their beards and eyebrows.
                                        What to do with Fatima.
She has done it again, worn
                              the red skirts to the market square.
          She says their thread and swish
                                        make her feel the villagers
open their doors and windows to her
                              as she steps into their footprints.
          God only knows what devil
                              has worn the skirts before,
what sly dancer, what ghost-woman
                              of the streets in what city
          in what final blue slice of night
                                        held against the rinse of dawn.

Everyone in the village knows
                    when Fatima passes
          the birds sing like silver,
                              and when she slips
into the baker's, the butcher's,
                    that last fresh loaf
          & thickest marbled cut
                              must be hers. As she passes
they whisper at her
                    their most secret desire and a quick look

into the dark of her eye

                         yields a shimmer of all things

possible. Fatima is called

                   to the better sky she sees from a high cliff

in a temple above an ocean

                        spilling itself over yellow sands.

The stones float down

               like storm clouds that will not reach her.

Each hardened palm releases

                    its own banishment under her spell.

BELLE ISLE

James River Island, site of the Confederate prison camp at Richmond

If saying makes it so—he thought it might—
he wanted to believe everything said in that whisper
of snow slipping through chafed branches,
the mottled grey and black branches, those shells
of clear shining lacquer, the red berries and green
holly sharp against ice-glazed brush. It was
a thin whisper of someone he should know,
unceasing. He had not expected beauty.
It was Belle Isle; beauty was not expected.
Still, it was true, he wanted to believe he might
go on marching, *one foot, one foot*, marching on
into something of hope, someplace
warm. But he was tired, tired and beyond
being cold, he wanted to sit down.

He could be quiet, it would be sudden
Christmas, he could be simply stopping
a moment to take in a quiet and fresh
snowfall in the wood, simply stopping a moment
on his way home, candles in each window
lighting the way home, one foot bundled
in rags, the other flopping in a torn boot,
the boot of a man shot as he ran for the river.
Or was it artillery that time, a canister blast?
But it was only a boot, a boot looking for its mate
as they marched away from him there where
he stood on one foot, the other gone to frost,

waiting at the road's edge, watching prisoners march
away around the bend into sheets of snow, turning
a page, shuffling '63 into '64 . . .

Then one foot one foot he was in the trees
and the straggling rear guard moved past
without a sound, entering nothing, nothing
but memory and hope ran away, hid her face,
the face of Eve, face of his sister,
face of one who listens, who knows
his dreams, his nightmares—the dream of a woman
lost among cones of purple flowers, the nightmare of a man
racing along walls of a purple maze—the sister who watched
over him as he chewed another of the dark berries,
nothing but raw turnips once in three days
but the purple berries had helped and were
helping, his tongue had swollen his throat shut,
he could not say prayer's first word, could
only sip a bit of cool air, whispering it in
even as the serpent had told Eve: *You will never die.*
The secret name of Eve has always been
Hope, and Hope will never die, sister whose soft voice
was there again now, no one else, whispering
no one else to see now or care, no one to miss,
and just then he could see how it might be

years from now in this place, could see a man
might come walking these woods, he might even be
grieving, a man who might think he hated his life,
grieving without any longer knowing why,
but a man with more than brush in his belly,
who would come across this place, stand here
a moment stopped on the path toward home,
the path of his own perfect escape, where he vanished
without a trace into windswept snow.
                                        I am
that man, and I walk Belle Isle, and there is
a cold spot I step into each time, and something
inhabits me there and has given me this to say.

And saying makes it so, and so we hesitate,
he thinks of how he never had a sister,
how I have always wanted a sister, a sister
with a name like Hope or Charity, and then he knows
all that will be coming after him, fearful
at this last beauty before he goes, but listening
as the branches, haloed in the weak sun, shake
in the light breeze, the scuffle and clack, waiting,
alone with it, the clear white skin and shining eyes,
the rubbed silk voice saying *it's all right now*,

whispering *right*, whispering *now* as he enters the wind.

WINTER SOLSTICE: OREGON HILL

The stars have been thinking of us,
but they haven't written, sorry, no time.
The thin grey sky is one long dull harangue
just trying to tell us what's good for us, but
really, it doesn't care. The cold wants to know
what you have in your pockets. It is waiting.
The cold gets all up in your face.

This may be how it is one morning
on the shortest day of the year
when the sun stops, mumbles, drops
its change, rubs its face, turns back for home.
But there is no home in that sky
the trees are combing, gathering wool,
looking for any sign the gods will be
coming back and haven't decided this time
to stay down south forever.
We all need to get our feet back on the ground.

A black dog roams the street, looking at himself
in every black patch of ice, licking it. We know
how it is, and give him a drink, but
we can't, no we can't, let him come inside.
Goodbye, Schubert, goodbye.

QUIPU OF THE SCORCHED LORD

Horse-men came with their barley beer and dust,
rum and flags, squeal of armor, stink
of wine, beatings they gave themselves
under the sun and inside the drizzle and gritty rain
with the *nine-tailed cat* and the black tarred
rope and the cane for the boy who must *kiss
the big gun's daughter*. Cruelty alights in power
without knowledge, and so it was without wonder
the black mouth would kill wherever it was
pointed. The long-faced conquerors sailed out
in the hiss and surge of their wooden belly's dark
laced with what was written in secret and sea foam
to fall upon the back of the promised land,
wolves in the eyes of the thousands of thousands
waiting to welcome the fevered dreams of men
who night and day would talk to their books and charts.
Buzzards rule where eagles have fallen from the sky.

The Inca was already at war, no time
for runners and their tales, warriors of steel
with impossible appetites, fiery gods
kept close as lovers sleeping,
the sudden blood. The Lord sent them
such presents, well-worked masks and useless
trinkets the white-faced hair-faced men wanted
to eat, ignorant of the rite of touching gold dust
to tongue. Wild men, lost, distracted and sick

with lust—the Lord sent young wives to calm
them, these angry ones, and sweet wives, too, for their
angry horses, which ate real corn, like real men.

When Atahualpa at last understood
they meant to burn him, he submitted instead
to be strangled so that his dried body might
live on as lightning among the Incas of the Incas.
They burned him anyway. *And* his ancestors.

Daily now the black-gowned priests drag
the ancestral mummies into the fire,
by night the people steal them back again,
lightning to parade the streets.

Broken by knives of flame, crushed
to dust at the hands of the wind,
the dry ancestors thirst for time and strength
the Jesus-priests have taken away to their distant
god to hang in the sky beyond the sea, their one god
white men have killed and raised from the dead
so they might kill him again. The white men nail endless
agony to a cross and make us kneel to kiss it.

Come back through the flames, we pray. Give us water
for our thirst, o Lord. In the dark of every eye you burn.

THREE

The relatively calm solar atmosphere can be torn asunder by sudden, brief outbursts called solar flares, the most powerful explosions in the solar system.

—NASA'S COSMOS, "THE VIOLENT SUN"

The beauty of the world is the mouth of a labyrinth. The unwary individual who on entering takes a few steps is soon unable to find the opening . . . he walks on without knowing anything or hoping anything, incapable even of discovering whether he is really going forward or merely turning round on the same spot . . . if he does not lose courage, if he goes on walking, it is absolutely certain that he will finally arrive at the center of the labyrinth. And there God is waiting to eat him.

—SIMONE WEIL

STRANGE CHILD

I was five and I ran away for no good reason
into the farthest field of my grandfather's farm.
The wheat: pale gold, barbed as my own
hair, taller than my eyes, blinding.

My grandmother and I had been wringing wet
clothes through the *watch your fingers!* mangle,
the next thing she knew I was
gone. The black dog vanished with me,
happy to go. That's how it was always
told in the grandmother story, how I was found:
with my white-gold hair and my three-foot height
I had disappeared into waves of grain. It was the dog
jumping up to look, that punctuation, that black dot.

So the story's sentence, laid down again, never quite
right. Perhaps I *was* running away, or
I was simply running, heading out
for the pond and its fat green frogs, the awful
snakes like question marks dangling in the willow, the fish
who slept under ice all winter, open-eyed.
Maybe it was the Thunder Moon hanging on
and fading like premonition in reflected morning sky.
Maybe I was answering a call. I could hear it then,
and I entered the gold field to roll away forever.

I couldn't know the field as a labyrinth.
Couldn't see as I whirled and ran into it,
couldn't sense the storm coming, the need
my grandfather had to bring in the wheat,
couldn't hear the combine's teeth chattering
in the field's far corner, couldn't understand
I had been raised by strangers who lied
for my sake, couldn't catch myself running deeper
to the place a person unknown was waiting
while the wheat rubbed itself to whispers
saying over the secret names: *Osiris, Orpheus,
Lemminkäinen . . . come here now boy, come here*
feeling the blades of wheat surge and slash
in the wind, cutting it to pieces, slicing it down
to some old words coming back, slashing at everything
I was, taking me apart, laying me down
in the dust and chaff among the slaughtered gods
and the children of gods. *He stepped into the gold
light, it slammed shut tight as a coffin, he felt the stinging
hatred of the water snake, he was torn to pieces
and scattered on the waters, he was singing like a fool*
already I was not like the others,
I was taking up names never heard before,
entering stories untold and singing them out
around me, forty years before I could find my way
into this, forty years before astronomers could find
at the center of every field of stars

a monstrous black mouth swallowing light and time,
swallowing itself, yet still starved, still trapped,
and so I was happy then, glad to lie down
and roll in the whispering leaves and stalks,
not like you or like them but as myself for once, flat
on my back at the center—slaughtered man-beast ready
for the woman to come and piece me together again.

BORGES IN THE LABYRINTH SUPREME

Another birthday, and *this* as his inheritance: black dust
swirling through the hourglass, black sand pouring into each
of the ten thousand jars of color. Yet one remains: a fierce orange.

Kodama will lead him on her arm deeper into the sharp
aroma that tightens his lungs and drives him down
through chill depths of stone—drilling into rock, into
the core of it, where the wind goes whistling inside.
Entering there takes him back, stone by back-stepping
stone, out over rough water, back to Dover,
the parchment-stiff curtain of powdered-wig cliffs
only she would have described that way for him and now
he laughs. He had asked what waited behind the curtain . . .

In every ending is another beginning.
He surrenders to the infinite loop of her
talk, they wander through Arabic, Icelandic—
while there, at the center of their winding walk,
waits the blinding surprise. In her voice he
senses it will be rare and knows it should offer
something more than beauty: the radiant power
of the lord of another realm.

The old magician was coming now at last
who had wandered so long, tracing his false
steps through layers of false worlds, dreaming
along the hidden iron bars, drifting among

the shallow pits, the paper-smooth
walls of the dungeons of comfort, the cobbled
walkways of delusion, the multiplying paths
which collect men from every corner
of the globe to be trapped here with him.

The smolder in that eye knew itself to be
the seventh incarnation of the tiger of Pindola,
the "tamed one" always pictured with the saint
riding his back or crouching at play.
Since the first spark had entered its body,
the tiger had never wanted another—
it always came back as the tiger. *Now*
this Borges was walking toward him
on the crisscrossing paths over disguised
bridges, past the small, unreal fields. This
Borges, master of illusion, priest of masks
and multiples in the mirror, fully entranced.

Later, wire photos will show the tiger
face to face with Borges, licking him, black claws
open in the great paw resting on his head.
It may be that what you see is the tiger
calmly considering how to eat Señor Borges.

Yet his muse will not accept his modest proposal.
She says: *marriage is not the best state; I don't believe in it.*
Beyond the seventh veil, there is a door: the lady *and* the tiger.

But just now in this moment's cascade, as they walk
arm in arm along their whispered way, they have not
arrived anywhere just yet, and if he pauses to wind the Swiss
movement on his wrist, it is so that the ritual of reluctance
might keep the thing frozen at its heart a mystery still
unknown, preserved as nothing more than exactly what
it has to be: a slow-winding spiral—something like
a string wound round and around on its post
tighter and tighter until at last it can be said
to *sing*.
          At its center roils the snarled sound
that hums in the cage of their ribs.
A god has trapped himself there and cries out.

Borges has been turning the story over in his mind:
in it, an eccentric dreaming couple mark their grave
and undulant progress—they follow an enormous syllable
along an eternity
               of scented paths through an oriental garden
where all the streams and fountains flow backwards,
reeling back the low sun as it wheels across the sky.

In that orange glow of what may be sunset or dawn or only
the color that lives beneath the lid of every closed eye,
the sound continues to grow around each turn, even as all the many
couples they might have been are glimpsed from behind exactly
when each of them disappears, arm in arm, turning down their other paths,
just as these two are turning into the couple they must be, which is
all of these impossible couples taken at once, singular
yet multiplied & undiminished, a final hammered chord that roars.

THE BLUE BREATH IN THE RED BRANCH

I am painting what you cannot see.

—David Freed

Whatever wind blows across that wintry branch turns it
red, setting loose a blue exhalation that trails off
like the last breath that broke down and gave way
inside the last word the old man could hardly whisper
when he saw everything was fire and vanishing,
and as he stood there, which is to say here, looking out
across the river in shock until the horses below hung their heads
and shook their harness, he could feel it burning into him
like a glowing iron brand, a knot he could never undo,
but when it released him he plunged down the bank,
jumped up into the wagon and took off into history

with a curse. Later that sour breath became a sparrow's chirp tangled
up in whatever I said the last frigid day we stood here, looking
into the same frothing waters he crossed back then, on the run
from his own pyramid of guilt and rage piled up heavy as stone,
running from where I stand again now among these Victorian and still
older stones on the cemetery bluff, keeping watch as a heron arrows
into the chill grey and black ducks skim down and geese round
the curve in this river I insist on calling my river and keep calling it
so, peace to Heraclitus and to you and to all of the dead who keep on
wanting to come back. This river, my river, burns with the weak coin
of pale winter sun and carries its lights without pause to the sea.

So I breathe my smoke into the ruined air that's made clean again
down inside the old trees and that wind is here, bending the branch
weighted with the breath of the man who died to lie buried here

beneath my feet, a man who in the end had nothing much himself
to say, no last sentence to carve into stone so that when the wind came
back like the cheated dead to blow out that breath trapped in the branch
and tear it open against his rock, the words not chiseled there
could neither hide nor disappear, even as the stone itself turned black.

Did that man have it right, *say nothing*, or is it that his words, and
mine, and yours are—*all together now, blow out the candles*—all
a shattering smoke in the wind that now chafes the branch and chafes
the branch again and rattles its last few leaves as if they were dice to be
shaken or *just some numbers* as you said then, looking down at the slab
like a shimmering door, your own breath a blue knife of smoke, sharp
as the scrape of a hand swiped at a frosted window so that we might see.

BESIDES

Those palominos, sweet doves, gallop here and never
draw any closer. My head hit the rock wall of the well—
Mister Little To Nothing knocked me in, if you need to know,
my *father*—and that was it. For a while I was thinking I was
thinking, then I wasn't. Like rats in the big barn.
Mouth foam, little beaches. Their vacation paradise.
The grain elevator man told me once rats can laugh.

So I died and it wasn't much different from anything
else, maybe it was too much like Nothing's shaky hand
scratching a line through each number on the funeral
home calendar, sending our days into the shit
hole of never never. And where was *what should have been?*
Labor from sunup, no breakfast till noon, beatings
the rest of the day—the neighbors' wild-eyed horses got
treated better, though they got their share of pain.

The last thing in my head, besides *I guess
it all had to come to this, old daddy of mine*
after the hammer landed and I was flying,
besides the blue shining all around my shadow
as I spilled into the cold and dark, shimmering
like a rainbow-coated starling swooping into the waiting
wheel of light, besides that last glimpsed ripple

of cream-gold waves ruffling the wheat field's hair
then the feel of it, wind on my face I carried with me
into the next world and the next: *Big nothing
comes from little to nothing you know, and
besides, I'm glad I poisoned the water.*

SOUTH AFRICAN
WOMAN OF 1986

Four days into her journey
she is tired beyond the burning
she has fed so long. The truck,
in which they chafe like livestock
pressed so close they lose control
of their bowels, is jolting her.
But not breaking, not
yet, not ever, she is telling
herself on the way to see
the brother who lives beyond
the face of the prison guard,
a rumor with guns bristling
on the wall edged with coiled
barbed wire that writes out
his name and is all we know
she will ever see of him again.
Blood breaks over the trembling
snarl of her lip caught in teeth
sinking deeper with each rut.
His knotted staff comes into her hand.
Now the walk begins, pain spreading
out into surfaces. Shadow-feet
in dust hot and white as coals.
Now the black plume in her headdress
makes an angry stab at every step,
a question she will ask again, shouting
out the name that is a spell

whose power shakily resurrects
smoked images of the unsmiling boy
who once gave her more than
half of the first apple
he had ever tasted. Fingers curled
in a chain link gate, she will softly
ask again, and be told another white
nothing. She will carry home
the bread she has baked for him.

In her dry mouth it is paper.
Written there, a name she eats.
She gives what is left to children
of the yellow homeland street, an odor
of rubber and flesh lingering there
where yesterday a woman was necklaced,
the gasoline in the Goodyear
scorching the face beyond recognition,
gnarled knob on a walking stick.
She pretends the hungered grateful look
in the children's eyes flared in his.
Light there fades quickly, hard
glints return, red with sunset glare.
Better perhaps than nothing, although
it's dirt, they say, that color.

APPROXIMATIONS IN ROMANTICS:
BENJAMIN ON HASHISH

after the 1931 experimental voyages of Walter Benjamin

When any someone has done something good, then well it may be
that good deed becomes the sharp eye of a bird. An eye that sees

so many more colors than we. When something evil, without doubt
that deed becomes the yellow eye of the goat. You've seen its black pupil:

that rectangular open-mouthed door swung wide for its glance to walk right
through you, fingering your things, probing your secret places. That's how it looks.

Perhaps one thoughtless morning you're even forced awake in the heavy
dew of a mountain meadow, say, in the Lake District, staring up astonished

at the ring of hairy faces murmuring purse-lipped around you an enchantment
opening the gates to a world of grotesques you refuse to enter. Soon it's worse

than how it looks even then. That evil grows, rings moving outward from the stone.
It becomes the evil eye of one's own cat, watching with lurid intensity

as you remove your underwear. Then the neighbor's dog, who won't stop
barking and barking your name like a dirty cough. Still, salvation is

possible. When something goofy is done, a man crawls back from the edge
of that girder above the Hudson. And if someone will *please pick that baby up*

and rub its back gently and bring it to sleep, the mountain will rinse
its cloudy hair in damp pearls of moonlight. And when any someone with dark

eyes and dark ringlets rolls her belly and shakes her hip in the empty bar
as if the Sultan watched every silver coin that's bounced on her hipbone, we

may each arrive home now to sleep all night without police banging at the door.
When any someone has kept awake & at work, even through the night bird's insane

chatter, a thin dawn again seals the protocols of our day. And when the rook flies
over, giving its sharp-tongued cry, the man staring at the ocean's mane may well forget

his sister's faceless murder, the shout of unbelieving terror he believes somehow
he should have heard, and her blond curls shake again with laughter uncontrolled.

ALIENS ARE CALLING US AWAY

All our stories are the same.

We only want that glass of stale water
to sit still by the bed, its idle bubbles
hanging there, holding our tired faces
mirrored & upside down like tiny bad

ornaments. We don't want that small ripple
to begin slowly whirling at its center,
then the wobble and jump when the water starts
to boil. None of us want that low hum, clouds streaming,

lightning without thunder, that draw into wind and night.

In the cone of pale blue light many of us
have been brought out, alone, to be lifted
up into the silenced chambers
of another kind of love.

All our stories are the same. We have a calling.
That one with the black liquid eyes
looks once and we cannot resist, we must follow
the urge dreaming us, drawing us out again

to have our legs parted,

our sex examined, our anus probed,
the cold insertions in our mouth and ears.
We are being used, our bodies taken
for the half-alien children we will never

understand, never be able to keep as our own
even if they hope to come back again
to this watery planet that swims
through the dark, the blue eye they cannot

forget, to catch us up and make us slaves,

to place us without a word
in the zoo without walls or windows,
the blank floor that might be
nothing. . . . And now here it is all over

again, he is here, eyes black as spilled ink,
spilled alien over the blank page to run wildly
into itself, ink chasing its tail, ink squirming
into such bent characters, black ink needing us,

knowing what we are, yet calling. Calling us away.

STRANDED

Our brothers and sisters are rising again.
You have seen & heard them—the ones who sing
for each other, who never cease making those songs
that tell who we are, where we began & have gone.

Their journey is long. Like Satan, displaced, they wander
to and fro, up and down in the burning sluice of its starry robe.
Their prayers are laced nets, their mute witness of scars
many and lasting, more than those of a Jonah or Job.

They are leviathan. But it is not enough, it is never
enough, and the wish surfaces in their song: to leave
behind the vast blue-black, depart forever the silent grey
fishes in their schooled swarms, the toothy writhe

of barracuda, the swift lunge of the shark, the rocking
plankton marshes, the jet & lash & terrible beaks of giant squid.
For it is never enough. They trumpet and moan
& plunge down and down in the heavy dark,

remembering. There, beyond the shoreline & its ragged
edge of stunted trees, there beyond the crumbling
lighthouse and the holiday hotels, they still sing
of the home they left long ago, dimly recalled,

a song of the green rolling valley,
the dark scented grove of hemlocks,

the winged seeds of the furrowed elm,
the bright grass and the many birds

in the far good place of their song.
They believe they might be birds again.
They wish to fly up into air—you've seen them
trying. But it's good they do not understand

as we stand beside them now, splash
a little water on their sides, stroke
their thick skins, sorrowful and confused
by our doomed and larger selves, & why

it must be this way. They cannot hear us
trying to explain the reason they have come.
They pay no attention to the ropes we lash
around them, our sad efforts to make them go.

Metaxis & nostalgia blur. We turn to dynamite,
bulldozers, towering cranes. Their eyes are closed,
they give us no mind. They are leviathan. They are
singing. Their journey is long.

ORACLE ON 42ND STREET

(ante Disney)

Could be rappers have it. A woman
is a hammer. Mahfouz says so now.
Oh it's a thoroughfare *in the heart of little old
New York* and friend Mahfouz drives a cab straight
into the cavernous night called Manhattan,
shows me to the street *where the underworld
can meet the elite.* He knows better
than the almighty where to find the best
Chinese or Greek, the last warm falafel,
the darkest corner where a whore will flip
her breasts from her tube top like headlights
staring over a cliff. Curious? He is always
knowing where it's at, and now it's this basement
full of ozone and sniff, charged with the toll
every mother's son will pay to be caught
loitering in the grasp of its smoky red light,
where *every move you make* pounding your head
will cost. Instantly Mahfouz disappears
somewhere laughing and I'm left to pull open
the first door that comes cold to my blind hand.

I am standing up like other men
staked in a circle, each one in his cramped
closet, the plywood coffins of a potter's field.
I take my place on the compass, slipping
quarters in, money to raise the dead
velvet curtain on the writhing couple, dead

center on the circular bed. What they manage
to do, I won't tell—unless you give me
a quarter—more than it's worth, I'm sure, to anyone
with an imagination.
                              Outside, in the outer circle,
more blank doors, things you do alone with more
silver in the slot. When the partition shoots up,
a figure before me in a bare glass cage,
a cloud of white hair, a black bra and thong
and impenetrable Gorgon stare who
picks up the phone, motions for me
to pick up my end in my small dirty room.
I have to kneel to hold the short-cord receiver
to my face, but she is a power in this world,
a mover and shaker, I know she will
tell me what I need to do. Like any god,
she sees me darkly, keeps it strictly
professional, she knows the way to release
the unspeakable secret in all mankind,
to get anyone to say it out loud,
to pray and swear and hammer
against the glass that keeps all the answers
out of reach. She asks it, simple and open,

What do you want?

She is breathing impatiently at the end
of the line, I am taking up her time
and wasting mine, I will have to pay
for this again. What do I want, for heaven's sake.
Drums thump, cymbals sizzle. A music, far.
She will offer anything my little heart
desires but soon this door, oh friend, will close.

I say it: *I want to know*
how to get out of this place.

She nearly smiles, her eyes are cold.
The snake raises its head to taste the air.
I try again.
           I want to know your secret name.

The shutter slams down, leaving me once more
to stand up in the dark like the man I am
with the taste of fear as iron on the tongue
and precious as a nail driven home.

A THANKSGIVING IN MOUNTAINS
WITH KENSEI AND WIND CHASER

after Miyamoto Musashi, samurai

No inner meaning yet no surface
in the *Ichi* school of the long sword—
only the warrior and his path.
No penance and no turkey, no guilt
and no gravy, no attachment, no cranberry

sauce. *In strategy, there is no interior and no gate,*
he wrote from his cave. *If you go into the mountains,*
and determine to go deeper and still deeper, you will emerge
instead back at the gate. The forest path
and the skeleton, the sloughed skin

and the underground spring. Wings fluttering
at my ear. How much solitude is required?
Mind has mountains. This year I will thank:
one path & one skin under November sky
letting down its red-gold hair and shimmer of lights

for my beloved dead to strike through with me,
stepping into every step I leave, filling each print
like rainwater, even as I take my thousand breaths,
hard & close, then far, so I may sing *hao hao*
up through the valley's dusty throat.

Musashi recommends the warrior stance,
sending strength into the hairline,
flaring the nostrils, head erect, eyes

narrowed, feet not close, not far apart.
Still, I bend to the waters' flashing mirrors.

The Way of the warrior does not include
other Ways, such as: Confucianism, esoteric
traditions, artistic accomplishments, dancing.
I confess to the dancing.
Musashi looks away to the mountain stream,

having written from his cave, *This is the truth:*
when you sacrifice your life, it is false
to die with a weapon yet undrawn.
I've got all I can handle, I tell his spirit.
From one thing, know ten thousand things.

Let's try this, I say. Never once did you lose
a fight, but to cross the stream each of us
must leap   stone to stone   over the deep
drum pounding down under the blue-green channel
as the river gives welcome to the branch just there

pouring in below the falls. A fire still lives
inside the wind that roars above in the stripped
hickories and white oaks. Seven hemlocks now, green
turning to dark, sentinels against the surging smoke-grey tide.
My mother is dead; brothers, dead; my father, vapor, and

my old flame is never coming back. *The Way of Walking*
Alone: when the clouds of bewilderment clear away, there is
the void. Blue Ridge, Sugar Hollow, the *Book of Five Rings*.
Four centuries annihilated in the lightning-bright slash
of my flowing sword—burned as the solitary taper of an afternoon.

THE VISIT: CLOUDS IN TROUSERS

Power saw ringing the end of its cut, hammer
Drumming its blunt obsession, driving it
Through heavy summer damp and murmur
Of voices snowing the globe of afternoon, and so
It begins. We approach as shadows in a ghostly fog—
Old Virginia clapboard farmhouse and fruit trees
Materializing in the yard, explosions of fat blue hydrangeas,
Magnolias towering over the stone path we follow
Into the menace & allure of slick dark leaves. We want
Simply to live here, perhaps once we did. Let's open
The screen door, step inside, yet no one is
Here, the house feels us enter & we feel it too, the absence
Of those who make this *home*, the children for whom
It will always be magic, the couple for whom
It will always be magic and trouble and now we must
Wonder, is this a dream? Such things don't matter
Anymore. The voices come again, we can't tell what
They're saying, and what they're saying doesn't
Matter, we don't want to understand, hold that
Off. We want to be here wavering with these tones
Hanging bells in the air. All we have wanted
And could not say, all we have lost without knowing,
Now belongs here to the strong young couple
Who hold within, tucked inside, that other couple
We once dreamt but could not keep alive. The scent
Of fresh-cut flowers and cooking and the warmth
Of late afternoon sun slips over us. Our puzzled expressions

Linger in the shadows, our dim proposals hang back
In the shadows and it seems they will never *come out*
Come out wherever you are into this pale hovering, yet now
Here they come, our friends & their children, arms
Open, mouths open, ready to shout and to kiss.

DIONYSUS WAITING

Theseus, that golden boy, has killed
    The Minotaur, and Ariadne has followed him—
Her bright thread under a sinking sky—
    Into the ship of black sails
And lost herself among the islands.

Dionysus is waiting.
    The songs have ended, the jeweled cup
Has tipped and drained. He has seen that
    Ariadne may not come to him in a lifetime.
Yet Dionysus is waiting, knowing what lies
    At the heart of every knot that binds
A space to a space, a man to a woman.
    He is alive in that, building
Its hollow amazements around him.

SLEEPWALKER IN THE
MEDICINE WHEEL

The spine snapped in two.
Showers of sparks—burning snowflakes—then out.
His rib-punctured lung . . .   Stop it.

                                     Start here.

No clouds, sun pouring into my face,
Sloshing the pulse with its flood of color.
The many miles gone carrying the weight
From this high place to home
Where my brother lies broken, the rain-black
Roof, slippery Sunday shoes: the story of his fall
Scribbled out, signed in stars wheeling unseen
Above these dropped stones. Tribal councils
Have decreed the long walk to this mesa—
Old rock, earth root, snow dust, stone spine
Among the Big Horns—rams off there, on watch.

Blackness in the mouth of their walking.

I have stepped in the ancestors' steps,
Walked for my brother under the hand
Of the sun to which I raise closed eyes
To ask again. I have no prayer bundle
But this bag of bones, this schooled
Skull & its clapper tongue, now still
And dumb and still they come, fire wheels
Whirling in the spoked sun, wheels of fire
Taking my brother where he must go,

Wheels within wheels spinning a cold flame,
Feather of soot each of us must hold, each dark
That shatters in that red tide. Time returns paralyzed
From before the light was born, the blood tide
Returns the sun. Tied to this chain link fence
Rattling around this mountain windblown wheel,
Prayer flags flap their wings for the far, stunted pines.

                              Little brother,
Nothing lifts. The connection gone dead,
The pulse burned out. We will never survive
That dark again, where you walked in your sleep
And I followed, saying nothing, where you spoke
In your sleep, and I answered. Buried in the heart
Of the wheel once was a buffalo skull, its sockets filled
With long grasses. Now it's blind & deaf and gone. Circling
Left, always moving with the sun, I go walking on.

BIOGRAPHICAL NOTE

Gregory Donovan is the author of *Calling His Children Home* (University of Missouri Press, 1993), which won the Devins Award for Poetry. His poetry, essays, and fiction have appeared in *The Kenyon Review*, *The Southern Review*, *New England Review*, *42opus*, *diode*, *Crazyhorse*, *Hayden's Ferry Review*, *Gulf Coast*, *Copper Nickel*, and many other journals, as well as in a number of anthologies, including *Common Wealth: Contemporary Poets of Virginia* (University of Virginia Press, 2003). Among other awards for his writing, he is the recipient of the Robert Penn Warren Award from New England Writers, as well as grants from the Virginia Commission for the Arts and fellowships from the Ucross Foundation and the Virginia Center for the Creative Arts. Donovan is a faculty member in Virginia Commonwealth University's graduate creative writing program, where he has often served as the Director of Creative Writing, and he is Senior Editor for *Blackbird: an online journal of literature and the arts*.